WRITTEN BY
JESS KEATING

NEW YORK TIMES BESTSELLING ILLUSTRATOR
PETE OSWALD

Set Your Alarm, SLOTH!

More Advice
for Troubled
Animals from
Dr. Glider

DOCTOR
GLIDER, MD

Orchard Books • New York
An Imprint of Scholastic Inc.

To all the adventurers who love and protect this
beautiful world and the creatures in it! —J.K.

For Matt. —P.O.

Library of Congress Cataloging-in-Publication Data available
ISBN 978-1-338-23989-8 • 10 9 8 7 6 5 4 3 2 1   21 22 23 24 25 • Printed in China   38 • First edition, September 2021
Pete Oswald's illustrations were rendered digitally using gouache watercolor textures. The text type was set in
Proxima Nova. The display type was set in KG What The Teacher Wants. Book design by Brian LaRossa.

It's another beautiful day and my patient list is full! Ready to help some animal friends? Away we go!
DOCTOR
GLIDER, MD

Welcome to the Arctic, Dr. Glider! No matter how far I swim, I can't see anything to eat. The water is too murky! Do I need glasses?
Use your melon, my magnificent **mammal** friend! You don't need to SEE your food to find it, you can HEAR it!
HELEN BELUGA
HUDSON BAY, CANADA

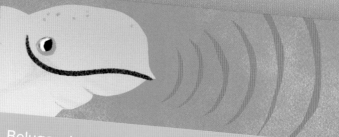

Beluga whales use **echolocation** to find food. This means they emit clicks and squeaks into the water, and listen for their echoes to return.

Belugas have a fatty deposit on their head called a melon. They wiggle their melon to direct sound in different directions.

Seriously? It's called a MELON?!

Yep!

By listening to where and how the sound echoes return back to them, belugas can figure out exactly where predators and prey are swimming.

You can't hide from me, fishy!

Many animals use echolocation to survive, including some bats, shrews, toothed whales, and even some cave-dwelling birds.

MONTY MARINE IGUANA
FLOREANA, GALÁPAGOS ISLANDS
ACHOO!! Dr. Glider! I can't — stop — SNEEZING! Am I sick? Do I have allergies?!

Fear not, my sea-faring friend! You aren't sick at all. Those startling sneezes are keeping you healthy. Just don't sneeze on your friends — that's gross!

Marine iguanas dive underwater to eat seaweed and **algae** on the rocks.

Because they eat underwater, these iguanas **ingest** a lot of salt water. Too much salt water can be very dangerous, so they've got to get rid of it.

A special **salt gland** in their faces does the job. These glands remove extra salt from their blood — then the iguanas just sneeze it out!

Salt glands are also found in some seabirds, **elasmobranchs**, and other reptiles.

My salt gland is near my butt!

SALT GLAND

ZOË ZEBRA
MASAI MARA NATIONAL RESERVE, KENYA
Flies, flies everywhere! They're driving me bananas, Dr. G — why do they keep dive-bombing and crashing into me?!

Sorry to break it to you, Zoë, but your stripes are confusing those flies! They can't help but crash your party!

Many biting flies carry disease and **parasites**, so animals must protect themselves.

Head-tossing, leg-stamping, and muzzle-flicking help **ungulates** like us get rid of flies!

Don't forget tail-swishing!

Flies target zebras, too, but in 2019, scientists discovered that they might be confused by their striking stripes!

Instead of landing on and biting zebras, flies often crash into them.

Mayday! HELP!

Humans sometimes use zebra-striped blankets to protect their horses.

Look at me, I'm a zebra now!

Isn't my nest the BEST, Chris?! The latest issue of *BETTER NESTS & GARDENS* says that red is the season's hottest color!
No way, Liam! Last night I watched *TWEET STREET*, and they said BLUE is the new red!
CHRIS AND LIAM THE SATIN BOWERBIRDS
SYDNEY, AUSTRALIA

Bowerbirds build elaborate nests called **bowers** to attract potential mates.

Some bowerbirds decorate their nests with brightly colored objects like berries, shells, leaves, feathers, rocks, and even bits of garbage or plastic.

Male bowerbirds will usually dance in front of their bowers, and females will mate with their favorite!

I told you boys before! All this chatter doesn't matter! Red or blue, do what's best for you!

Check out my moonwalk!

No! Pick me! I've got STYLE, baby!

OCTAVIA OKAPI
DEMOCRATIC REPUBLIC OF CONGO, AFRICA
RUMBLE!
RUMBLE!
Dr. G — you've got to set the record straight. I keep hearing these rumbly-tumbly sounds everywhere I go. Is it all in my head? Am I hearing voices?! HELP!

Oh, Octavia. Of course it's all in your head, but that doesn't mean you're making it up! That's your family you're hearing. They've got superpowers, and so do YOU!

Okapis use many sounds to communicate, including grunts, coughs, bleats, and whistles.

Okapis can also produce **infrasonic sounds**. These sounds are impossible for many other animals (including humans!) to hear.

These infrasonic sounds are very low **frequencies**, and help the okapis talk to each other through their dense forest homes.

In order to listen to okapi language, humans must use special computer programs that record and play the sounds.

DOCTOR GLIDER, MD

Dr. Glider, tragedy has struck! Our beloved clownfish queen has disappeared! Our school is in chaos, and with no one to lead us, we are destined to swim in circles forever!
I'm sorry for your loss, Clint, but it's your time to shine! Take charge!
CLINT CLOWNFISH
GREAT BARRIER REEF, AUSTRALIA

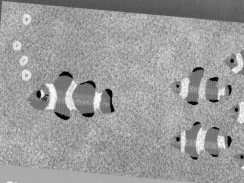

Clownfish groups are organized into a **hierarchy**, with a single female fish in charge.

This dominant female fish is often the largest of the group, and she gives orders to the rest of the fish.

If the female in charge of the group dies, the highest-ranking male fish will quickly transform from male to female. Now she is the leader!

My first order: WE SWIM AT DAWN!!

Many fish, gastropods, and plants are able to transform like this.

Grumble, grumble, roil, and trouble! Dr. G, what's up with these sounds in my belly?! I'm not even hungry!
My dear crustacean, I get your frustration! There's nothing wrong with you. Your tummy teeth are just talking!
GREG THE GHOST CRAB
NANTUCKET, MASSACHUSETTS

Many crustaceans have a specialized stomach called a **gastric mill** to help them digest their food.

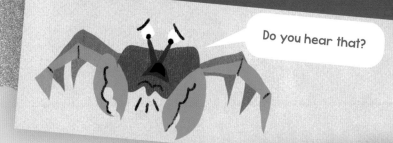

Do you hear that?

GASTRIC MILL

The gastric mill has strong muscles that help break down chunks of food. It's like a second set of teeth in their stomachs!

Scientists have learned ghost crabs also use these grinding noises to defend themselves when disturbed.

Back off, Bruce!

Run away!!

Ghost crabs also have specialized ridges on their claws and arms. By rubbing them together, they can communicate.

These sounds are called **stridulations**.

SAMLO SNOW LEOPARD

LADAKH, INDIA

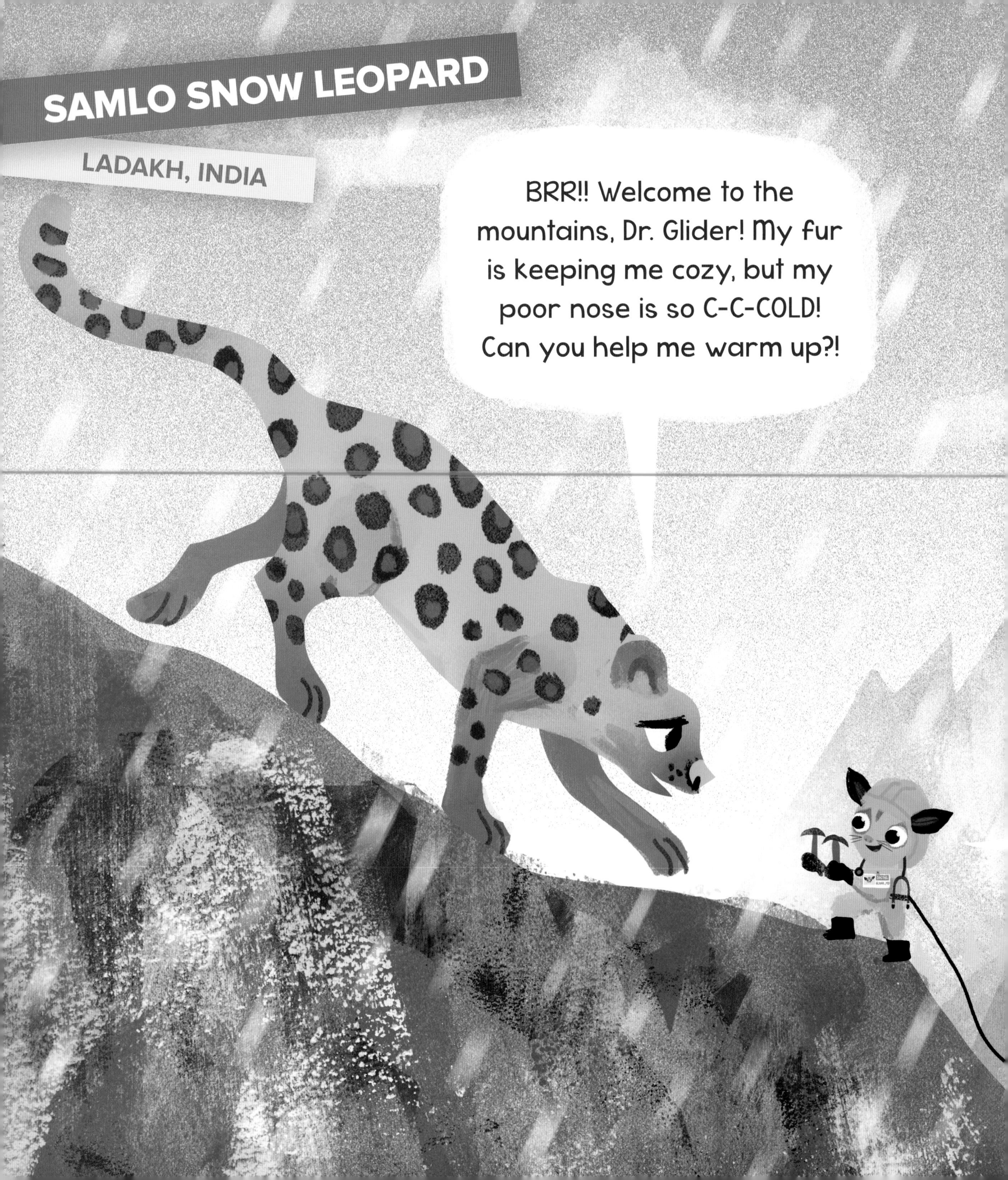

Snow leopards live in rugged mountain ranges, where the air is extremely cold and dry.

That's way too cold for me!

I'll take the sunshine instead!

They have thick fur to protect them from the cold. But their noses still get chilly!

To keep their noses warm, snow leopards curl their long, fluffy tails around their faces.

I'm snug as a bug . . . uh, leopard!

Snow leopards' tails are also used for balance when they run and jump.

My tail is almost as long as my body!

Show-off.

Silly Samlo — you don't need my help! You have an un-BRRR-lievable built-in scarf. Your tail will keep you toasty!

The grass is always greener on the other side of the sloth, Sabrina. You sleep so much that algae has grown on your back! Set your alarm, sloth — it's time to rise and shine!

Sloths are the slowest mammals in the world. They eat slowly. They move slowly. They even POOP slowly.

I only climb down my tree once a week to poop!

Sloths also sleep A LOT — sometimes more than fifteen hours a day in **captivity**! Because of their slow lifestyles, gardens of algae can grow on their backs.

This type of algae only grows on sloths!

It's a perfect home for some moths like me, beetles, and fungi!

While they forage for food, their green backs act as camouflage in the trees. Harpy eagles and jaguars are always looking for a meal!

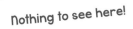

Nothing to see here!

SACHI THE PARADISE FLYING SNAKE

INDONESIAN ARCHIPELAGO, INDONESIA

Doctor, I am so exhausted, I'm afraid of falling out of my tree! The **canopy** here is so tall, it takes me hours to get to the top! None of my snake buddies are tired; what's wrong with me?

Wait. Are you telling me that you've been slithering all this time?! You are built for the skies! Take the leap, flatten your body, and glide!

Despite their name, flying snakes can't actually fly. But they *can* glide!

As they leap from the trees, flying snakes flatten their bodies. This helps them catch the air, similar to a parachute.

By **undulating** their bodies side-to-side, flying snakes can make sharp turns in the air.

There are only five known species of flying snakes. Some scientists think they are even better gliders than flying squirrels and other gliding mammals!

Wait, WHAT?! Even better than ME?!

Dr. Glider, I'm in LOVE! Isn't she gorgeous? There's only one problem: She won't talk to me. How can I woo this lovely lady?
WALT THE GREAT EGRET (WITH THE WHITE EGRET ORCHID)
PADANG, SUMATRA

Great egrets are known for their graceful stature and beautiful white **plumage**.

In **breeding season**, adult egrets will grow long feathers on their backs. These extra **adornments** are used in mating displays.

To woo females, males will preen their wings, bob their heads, and shake twigs in their bills.

White egret orchids are flowers, but they do look a lot like great egrets — they're even named after them!

Alas, my love, we are not meant to be!

Oh dear. It's not in your power to woo that flower! I mean, like, literally — that's a FLOWER, Walt. Maybe try your own species next time, okay?

BENNY THE BLUE DRAGON

KAUAI, HAWAII

It's your lucky day, Benny. Other creatures would get sick from eating a venomous creature like that, but you're built for it. Bon appétit, little blue dragon!

Blue dragons are a type of sea slug called a **nudibranch**.

We are **pelagic** animals . . .

That means they live in the open ocean!

Many animals stay away from the **lethal** Portuguese man o' war, but not blue dragons!

My tentacles cause painful stings! Muwahaha!

Blue dragons can eat these stinging tentacles. Instead of getting hurt, their bodies move the stinging cells into their own skin.

By stealing these cells, blue dragons become venomous themselves. If you ever spot one, don't touch it!

KOKO THE KOOKABURRA

CAPE YORK PENINSULA, AUSTRALIA

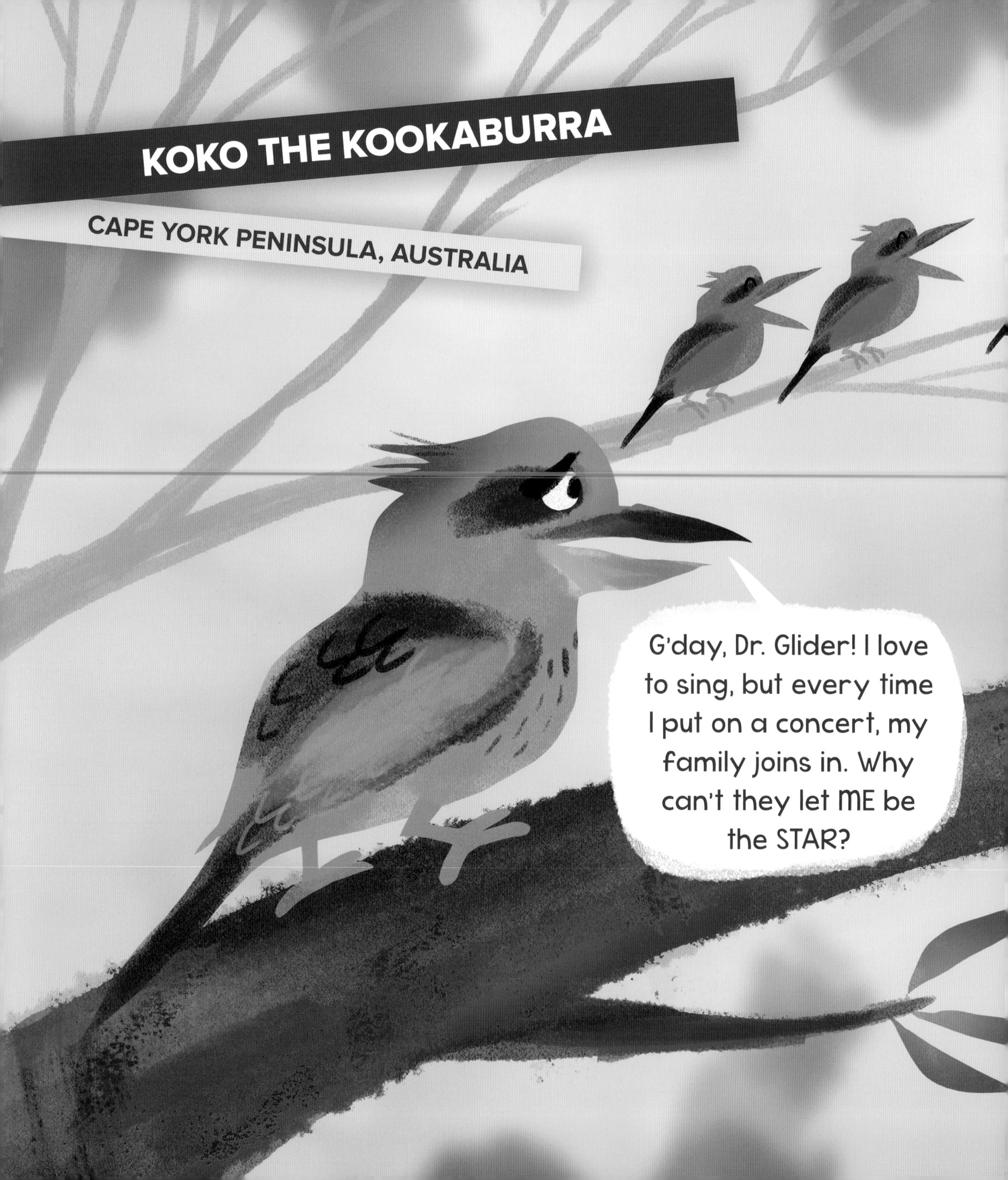

Kookaburras have unique and very distinctive calls that sound like loud chuckles, trills, hoots, and laughter.

Ooohahahahahhaha!

What are they laughing at?!

Along with singing at dawn and dusk, kookaburras also have calls to signal danger, announce their territory, ask for food, find others, and court mates.

When one kookaburra in a family starts to sing, others will usually join them!

OOOHAHAHAHHHAHAAHAHHA

There they go again.

Like many birds, these noises arise from a vocal organ in their chests called a **syrinx**.

I'm the reason birds can sing!

Oh, sweet Koko. You're already a star! Birds of a feather sing together — you and your family will be pitch-perfect!

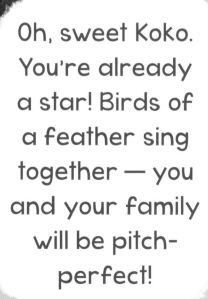

DOCTOR GLIDER, MD

RUBY AND REMY REINDEER

MACKENZIE DELTA, NORTHWEST TERRITORIES, CANADA

Fear not, Ruby! Reindeer eyes change color with the season, so you're always in style. Haven't you checked your reflection? Your eyes turned blue, too!

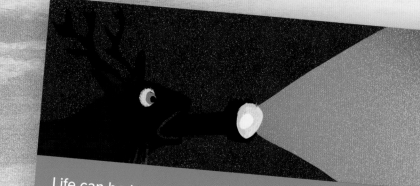

Life can be tough in the Arctic. Sometimes, it stays dark for twenty-four hours!

Reindeer have a special **adaptation** to cope with darker days. Their eyes change from gold to frosty blue!

Blue reindeer eyes are about one thousand times more sensitive to light than gold ones. This change helps them see better in the dark winters.

Groovy.

In summer, their gold eyes help to bounce sunlight away from their eyes. This is like a natural pair of sunglasses!

About Dr. Sugar Glider

Dr. Sugar Glider is a sugar glider who was born and raised in eastern Australia. Her parents encouraged her love of science at a young age, and she was the only creature in her tree who learned to read and write. She studied zoology at the prestigious Oxford University (the only sugar glider in her year to do so), and enjoys climbing trees, reading, and of course, helping her fellow animals live healthy and happy lives. You can find more about her at www.jesskeatingbooks.com/drsugarglider.

The library is one of my favorite places! To learn more about the amazing animals of the world and how to protect their homes, visit your local or school library. Tell them Dr. Sugar Glider sent you!

Words to the Rescue

▶ **adaptation:** a process of changing over time, to better fit into one's environment

▶ **adornments:** characteristics on an animal that serve a decorative function

▶ **algae:** simple, nonflowering plants that use light and chlorophyll to make food

▶ **bowers:** shelters made by some species of bowerbirds

▶ **breeding season:** a season of the year in which animals mate

▶ **canopy:** the top layer of a forest, formed by mature trees and other organisms

▶ **captivity:** a condition of being confined in a space

▶ **crustacean:** a class of mostly aquatic animals with hard exoskeletons, jointed legs, and segmented bodies

▶ **echolocation:** a process of using sound waves to locate objects

▶ **elasmobranchs:** a group of animals with skeletons made of flexible cartilage (including sharks, skates, and rays)

▶ **frequency:** the rate at which a sound wave vibration occurs

▶ **gastric mill:** a specialized stomach in some animals used for grinding up food

▶ **hierarchy:** a system in which organisms are ranked one above the other according to status

▶ **infrasonic sounds:** sound waves that are below the range at which a human ear can hear

▶ **ingest:** to eat or drink

▶ **lethal:** capable of causing death

▶ **mammal:** a class of warm-blooded animals with fur or hair, a skeleton, and glands that produce milk for their babies

▶ **nudibranch:** a type of soft-bodied marine mollusk without a shell

▶ **parasite:** an organism that lives on or in another organism (called its host) and that takes nourishment from that organism

▶ **pelagic:** relating to the open sea or ocean

▶ **plumage:** a bird's feathers

▶ **salt gland:** a gland that secretes excess salt

▶ **stridulation:** the act of producing sound by rubbing together certain body parts

▶ **syrinx:** the voice organ in many birds

▶ **undulating:** a wave-like motion

▶ **ungulates:** mammals with hooves

▶ **venomous:** capable of secreting venom, and injecting it with a bite or sting

Dr. Glider's

Ptilonorhynchus violaceus **Satin bowerbird**

Amblyrhynchus cristatus **Marine iguana**

Delphinapterus leucas **Beluga whale**

Okapia johnstoni **Okapi**

Equus quagga **Common zebra**

Amphiprion bicinctus **Red Sea clownfish**

Ocypode quadrata **Ghost crab**